Contents

What Can You Do?

 HOUGHTON MIFFLIN   BOSTON

Printed in China

ISBN-13: 978-0-618-93195-8
ISBN-10: 0-618-93195-3

1 2 3 4 5 6 7 8 9 SDP 15 14 13 12 11 10 09 08

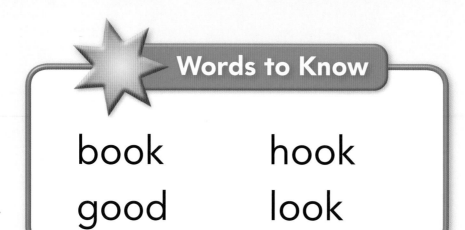

book   hook

good   look

afraid   tall

Bear   water

My Pictures

by Gus Gedatus

illustrated by Phyllis Harris

Come look at my pictures!
Come see.
See how funny a picture
Can be.

Bear swings from a hook,
While Cat reads a good book,
And Mule sings a tune
For a bee.

Dog slides on a water slide.

He squeals!

He's afraid of the duck

On three wheels.

My tall, yellow goat
Has a red and green coat.
She took a long ride
With a seal!

Words to Know

backpack

crosswalk

dumptruck

mailbox

any   most

follow   tall

idea

What I Do

by Gus Gedatus

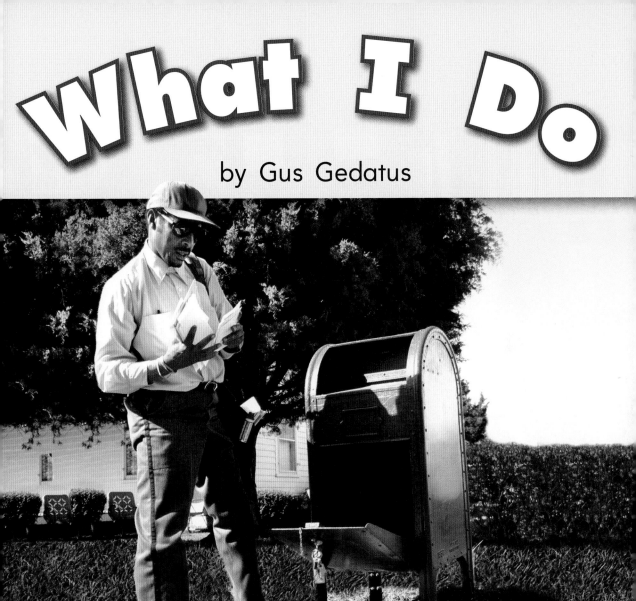

Who has any mail to send?
Most mail can go in a mailbox.
Then I pick it up.

Who needs books to read?
I have an idea. I'll help fill
your backpack with books!

Who needs to cross the
street? Wait at the crosswalk.
Follow me!

Who needs lots of rocks?
I drive a dumptruck. I can help!